MAR 2 7 2018

BUILD YOUR BUSINESS

START YOUR PET-SITTING BUSINESS

by Tammy Gagne

CAPSTONE PRESS
a capstone imprint

Snap Books are published by Capstone Press
1710 Roe Crest Drive, North Mankato, Minnesota 56003
www.mycapstone.com

Library of Congress Cataloging-in-Publication Data
Names: Gagne, Tammy, author.
Title: Start your pet-sitting business / by Tammy Gagne.
Other titles: Start your pet-sitting business
Description: North Mankato, Minnesota : Capstone Press, [2017] | Series: Snap
   books. Build your business | Audience: Ages 8–14. | Audience: Grades 4 to
   6. | Includes bibliographical references and index.
Identifiers: LCCN 2016047901| ISBN 9781515766896 (library binding) | ISBN
   9781515767015 (ebook (pdf)
Subjects: LCSH: Pet sitting—Juvenile literature. | Money-making projects for
   children—Juvenile literature. | New business enterprises—Juvenile
   literature. | Entrepreneurship—Juvenile literature.
Classification: LCC SF414.34 .G34 2017 | DDC 636.088/7—dc23
LC record available at https://lccn.loc.gov/2016047901

EDITORIAL CREDITS

Editor: Gena Chester
Designer: Veronica Scott
Media Researcher: Kelly Garvin
Production Specialist: Laura Manthe

PHOTO CREDITS

Shutterstock: alexmillos, 20, andyOman, 7, Blend Images, 8, Chutima Chaochaiya, 3, 31, Djem, 1 (left), Eric Isselee, 1 (right), 4, 19, Ermolaev Alexander, 23 (bottom), gillmar, 1 (top), GiselleFlissak, 13, glenda, 9, Grzegorz Placzek, 22, Guas, 21, Halfbottle, 11, Happy monkey, 10 (b), Inna Astakhova, 25 (top), Irina Kozorog, 23 (t), LaraP, 28, Michelle D. Milliman, 24, Nadezhda Bolotina, 2, 30, 32, nelik, 5 (b), Nelja, 25 (b), NotarYES, 5 (t), Olivier Le Moal, 29, Paul Hakimata Photography, 14, pjmorley, 15, PhotoMediaGroup, 16, Rawpixel.com, 10 (t), Satawatch Katlivong, 17, Sergey Novikov, 27, tenenbaum, 18, tomertu, 26, Tyler Olson, 6, Viacheslav Nikalaenko, 12, Yuliya Evstratenko, cover
Artistic elements: Shutterstock: Art'nLera, grop, Marie Nimrichterova, Orfeev

Printed and bound in China.
004725

Table of Contents

Is Pet Sitting for You?

Imagine getting paid to spend time with animals! Playing with energetic dogs and petting silky cats are just a few of the ways pet sitters spend their workdays. Of course, pet sitting is not all fun and games. Pet sitters also feed, walk, and clean up after animals. But even these more serious parts of the job can be fun for animal lovers. If you like animals, this type of business can be a great way to earn money.

Caring for pets is a big responsibility. Perhaps you have dogs or cats of your own. If so, you may care for them every day. This experience can make you an ideal pet sitter. Even if you don't have pets yourself, you can learn how to care for animals professionally.

Pet sitters need many things to run a successful business. A few basic supplies and an advertising plan will help. But the most important requirements are a love of animals, a positive attitude, and a commitment to care.

Do Your Homework

It is important to know as much as you can about the animals in your care. Perhaps you have family members or friends with pets. Ask if you can spend some time helping them with their animals. Doing so will help you build useful experience.

Learn about specific breeds by reading about them. For example, Boxers need more exercise than Basset Hounds. Some cat breeds, such as the Abyssinian, enjoy playing fetch! The more you know about your clients' pets, the more valuable you will be as a pet sitter.

CHAPTER 1
GETTING STARTED

Before you start booking pet-sitting jobs, make sure you have all the necessary supplies. While your shopping list will not be long, each item is important for your success. You probably won't use every one for each job. But you will be glad you are prepared as the needs arise.

Even if you care for an animal in its home, it's wise to bring along basic cleaning supplies. Cleanup rags for accidents and pet wipes could come in handy. Slip them into your bag, and you will never be caught unprepared.

Keep a **slip lead** with you at all times. This simple device works as a one-size-fits-all collar and leash for any dog or cat. Use this as a backup when you can't find the owner's leash or when one hasn't been provided.

Pet-Sitting Survival Kit

Keep the following items on hand at all times so you are ready for your next pet-sitting job:

- cleanup bags
- first-aid kit
- folding bowl
- pet wipes
- slip lead
- full water bottle

Some items, such as leashes and water bottles, will last a long time. But you will need to restock others, such as cleanup bags and pet wipes, from time to time. In the beginning you may not be able to buy more supplies until you have earned some money from your pet-sitting sessions. As you take on more clients, plan regular trips to a pet supply store for this purpose.

Tip

Buy a calendar or planner to organize your schedule. Then you'll be able to keep track of all of your pet-sitting appointments.

slip lead—a leash that also serves as a collar when it is placed around an animal's neck

Advertising Your Business

Businesses must advertise their products and services. Your pet-sitting service will be no different.

Word-of-Mouth Advertising

One of the most powerful forms of advertising is word of mouth. This is when clients who are pleased with their service recommend a business to their friends.

It is also smart to introduce yourself to other business owners. When pet owners need sitters, they often ask their veterinarians, groomers, or local humane societies for recommendations. Visit these establishments to ask them to mention you if any customers ask for a pet sitter.

In order for word-of-mouth advertising to work, a business must have a good **reputation**. To build one, you must honor your commitments. Showing up on time and completing all the tasks assigned to you are important in accomplishing this goal.

Tip

Build your reputation through volunteer work. Consider donating some time to your local animal shelter. It is also an excellent way to learn more about caring for animals.

reputation—a business's character as judged by their customers

Marketing Materials

Hook clients by passing out materials that advertise your business. But make sure you get your parents' permission before you do, as marketing materials often display contact information.

Business Cards

Business cards are great marketing materials. Printing cards on your own will save money. Keep the design simple. Include your name and contact information along with the term "Pet Sitter." You may want to add a cute picture or a logo as well. This image will help people associate you with animals. Business cards make it easier for clients to get in touch when they need your services.

PROFESSIONAL
Pet Sitter
KATIE PARK: 555-3091

Flyers

You can also make flyers to advertise your business. Flyers should contain basic information including types of animals you care for and qualifications. You can even add **testimonials** from previous clients. Consider including pull-off tabs at the bottom with your name and phone number. As people discover your flyer, they can then rip off one tab at a time. As soon as all the tabs have been taken, post a fresh flyer with new tabs.

After making some copies, ask local businesses if you may display them. Pet-related businesses are ideal spots for this type of advertising, but any place where pet owners might shop can also help you reach new clients. Some businesses have bulletin boards for people to advertise community events. Always ask permission before adding your card or flyer to one of these spaces.

Offer Discounts

Reward your clients for spreading the word about your business. For example, offer them a 25 percent discount for their next pet-sitting session each time they send a new client your way. You could even offer a free session after a certain number of **referrals**.

Reward clients for repeat business. Consider offering a special deal for clients who book more than one pet-sitting session in advance. Two booked appointments could mean a 25-percent discount. Offer 50 percent off for three appointments.

Tip

Be sure to answer your phone calls and check your e-mails after handing out or posting any printed advertising materials. If you miss a call, return it promptly. This shows potential clients that you are responsible.

testimonial—an expression of appreciation or gratitude
referral—a recommendation given from an existing client to a new one

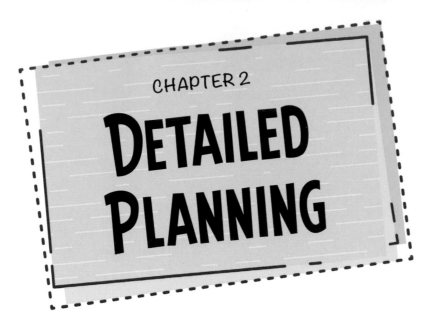

CHAPTER 2

DETAILED PLANNING

The most successful businesses follow a plan. Figure out what your rate should be before you take a job. Will you charge by the hour or by the pet? Will your fee be higher for dogs than for cats? There are no wrong answers to these questions. But it's important to use the same standards for each client. Setting your fees ahead of time makes the process easier on everyone.

Setting Your Fees

Not sure what your fee should be? Begin by setting a standard fee for pet sitting a single animal. This amount may be a daily or an hourly rate. Some pet sitters who charge by the hour charge a minimum of four hours.

You may charge a bit more for caring for a dog, since dogs likely need more attention. Next, choose a standard fee for a second animal. This fee may be a bit lower than the first. For example, you might charge only half the standard fee for each additional pet.

Tip

If you've agreed to accept checks as payment, you'll probably have to set up your own bank account. Ask your parents to help you set up an account for this purpose.

The First Meeting

Before you book a pet-sitting appointment, have a phone conversation with a potential client to work out needed details. Information that needs to be shared includes pay rate and a general description of the job. During the phone conversation, suggest a quick meeting. At the meeting, write down key information. It's easy to forget whether an animal gets a third-cup or a half-cup of food at each meal. Keep a checklist with notes to make sure you don't overlook an important detail.

Always check with your parents before visiting a new client. Your mother or father may even want to go with you. This first step provides an excellent opportunity to meet the pet and work out job details with the client.

Keep in mind that some owners may have special requests. If a pet requires special attention, make sure you are aware of this before the first appointment. Ideally, you should go over these requests with the client at your first meeting.

Be sure you have the phone number of the client's veterinarian before the start of each pet-sitting session. You should also know how to get in touch with your client in an emergency situation. Keep all important phone numbers handy at all times.

Tip

When meeting a new client, remember to greet the pet as well. A good relationship with the animal is essential to your success as a sitter.

Paperwork

Contracts are important for any service business. They ensure that both the service provider and the client have the same expectations. You can use a basic pet-sitting contract that can be changed slightly for each individual client. The contract lists the duties expected of you and should be signed by both parties before the job begins. Details in the contract will vary from one client to another. For example, some owners expect their dogs to be taken out on walks. Others expect their pets' designated potty spots to be cleaned up.

Make sure to list your agreed fee in the contract. This will prevent catching anyone by surprise later. You should also determine when and how you will be paid.

Cancelation Policies

Create a cancelation policy, and place it into your contract. Some pet sitters ask for a non-refundable **deposit**. If the client then cancels the appointment without appropriate notice, the pet sitter is allowed to keep the money. Likewise, a pet sitter should only cancel an appointment because of a sickness or if there is an emergency. In these situations, the pet sitter would return the client's deposit.

Tip

Print two copies of each contract. After you and the pet owner sign them, keep one and leave the other copy with your client.

contract—a written agreement stating the terms by which one will work for the other

deposit—a fraction of a payment given before a job is done

CHAPTER 3
SERIOUS RESPONSIBILITIES

Whatever tasks you agree to perform, you must follow through with them completely. Meals and walks should take place at the agreed-upon times. And you must clean up after the pet.

The owner may agree to let you do your homework, watch television, or other activities while you pet sit. Be sure these things don't interfere with your duties. If you are worried that you may forget to perform a certain task on time, set a reminder. Alarms can be especially helpful if you are caring for multiple pets.

REMINDER

7:00am

Walk Dogs!

Attitude is Everything

People enjoy dealing with others who are friendly and polite. Good manners go a long way in forming good relationships between you and your clients.

Keep a positive attitude with your clients and their pets even if your pet-sitting session doesn't go as well as you planned. A positive outlook helps to create a positive reputation for your business. This will encourage clients to book future pet-sitting appointments with you. It will also make your clients more likely to recommend you to other pet owners.

CHAPTER 4

WORK THROUGH PROBLEMS

Success in business can sometimes be tricky. But with preparation, determination, and dedication, your business has a good chance of achieving its goals.

Collecting Payments

Most of your clients will pay you for your services promptly without being asked. Some clients, however, might need a gentle reminder.

When your client returns home, you can use the contract as a way to start the conversation. Simply pick up the document and flip to the page that includes the balance due. Tell the client, "Let's see what we agreed on as payment for today's session."

Remain polite when requesting payment. Always say please and thank you. A client may ask to send a check or have you pick one up at a later time. Be flexible. If the client does not follow through with this arrangement, send a bill for the overdue amount. If you still don't receive your payment, talk to your parent or a trusted adult.

Dealing with Messes

Even the best-behaved animals sometimes have a variety of accidents. If the pet you are caring for has a house-training mishap, don't punish the animal in any way. Simply clean up the mess as quickly as possible.

Some accidents have nothing to do with house training. Cats are masters at knocking over plants or decorative items. But dogs can bump things over too. If a household item gets broken, do your best

to clean up. Dirt from a plant can go right back inside the pot. Any broken glass or sharp objects should be thrown away or recycled carefully and promptly. Otherwise, you or a pet could become injured. Always notify the owners about an accident upon their return.

Tip

Puppies need to relieve themselves often. Take a pup to its potty spot about 20 minutes after a meal and immediately following a nap or play session.

Other Problems

Sometimes, even with careful planning, your pet-sitting session won't go as planned. When problems arise, it's important to remain calm. Think quickly, critically, and creatively about the problem. Ask yourself why the problem is happening and how you can fix it.

Puppies can be especially challenging. If a puppy is fussing, first try to make sure that the pup has everything it needs. Check the water bowl. Take the pup to its potty spot for a chance to relieve itself. If there is no obvious reason for the fussing, try to distract the animal with a treat. You could also try talking to the pup softly or singing to it to comfort it.

If a pet seems set on trouble, try to distract it with play or exercise. A tired animal is much less likely to get into **mischief**. But just in case, move items that the animal can chew on out of reach.

Tip

If a puppy cannot be trusted to wander around the house by itself, use a leash as a **tether**. Hold onto the leash or hook one end to a secure post. This will reduce the pup's chances of getting into trouble.

mischief—playful behavior that may cause annoyance or harm to others
tether—a line that when tied between two things limits one's range of movement.

CHAPTER 5

WHAT COMES NEXT

Even small businesses require planning for the future. Perhaps you want to acquire a certain number of clients by the end of your first year. Or maybe you want to start caring for a greater variety of pets. Either way, set goals to help your pet-sitting service grow over time.

Most new businesses set a goal to break even their first year. This means that they make back the money that they've invested in the business during that time. You may have borrowed the startup money for your pet-sitting service from your parents. If this is the case, you could set an additional goal of paying them back after your first three jobs.

YEARLY GOALS:

1.

2.

3.

4.

Bringing in Help

One way you can expand your business is by hiring one or more other people. A single person can only book so many appointments. But you could serve more clients by working with others.

Make sure you hire the right people to help you. While it might be tempting to hire a friend, your clients should be your top priority. Employees should be dedicated and able to provide quality service.

Hiring employees to work for you is a big responsibility. Decide how your employees will be paid. Perhaps you will offer them half of each appointment's fee they work. Organization, communication, and team building skills all come together to ensure your business grows successfully.

Tip

Working with others can sometimes be difficult, and feelings can be hurt. Treat your employees the way you would like to be treated.

27

Invest in Yourself

Grow your business by investing more time and money into it. Expand the kinds of services you offer your clients. Offer to watch different types of animals, board pets at your home, or start to offer dog-walking services.

Clients who feel appreciated will be more likely to book more pet-sitting appointments with you. Consider investing some of your money in a bunch of pet toys to give clients as thank-you gifts, especially around holidays or for pet birthdays.

You can also make your business more successful by investing more of your time. Learn as much as you can about pets. Take a dog training class or a course in animal first aid. The more knowledge you have about animals, the more valuable you are to clients.

Get Certified!

The National Association of Professional Pet Sitters (NAPPS) is an organization that helps educate pet sitters. You must pay a fee and pass a test to become a **certified** member of NAPPS.

If you are certified, be sure to say so on your advertising materials. You can also mention your certification when meeting with a client for the first time. Many people will feel more comfortable leaving their pets with someone who is qualified.

Tip

Consider setting aside about one-third of every payment for supplies and advertising costs.

Starting and running a pet-sitting business is a lot of work. It will take commitment and determination. But from the pride of a job well done to the love for the animals in your care, its success has many rewards.

certified—having officially recognized training, skills, and abilities

Glossary

certified (SUR-tuh-fyd)—having officially recognized training, skills, and abilities

contract (KAHN-trakt)—a written agreement stating the terms by which one will work for the other

deposit (dih-PAH-zuht)—a fraction of a payment given before a job is done

mischief (MISS-chif)—playful behavior that may cause annoyance or harm to others

referral (ri-FUR-uhl)—a recommendation given from an existing client to a new one

reputation (rep-yoo-TAY-shuhn)—a business's character as judged by its customers

slip lead (SLIP LEED)—a leash that also serves as a collar when it is placed around an animal's neck

testimonial (TESS-tuh-mohn-ee-uhl)—an expression of appreciation or gratitude

tether (TETH-er)—a line that when tied between two things limits one's range of movement

READ MORE

Bacon, Carly J. *Cat Care: Nutrition, Exercise, Grooming, and More.*
Cats Rule! North Mankato, Minn.: Capstone, 2016.

Hyde, Natalie. *What Is Entrepreneurship? Your Start-Up Starts Now!*
A Guide to Entrepreneurship. New York: Crabtree Publishing, 2017.

Sutherland, Adam. *Be a Young Entrepreneur.* Hauppauge, N.Y.:
Barrons Educational Series, Inc., 2016.

INTERNET SITES

FactHound offers a safe, fun way to find Internet sites related
to this book. All of the sites on FactHound have been researched
by our staff.

Here's all you do:
Visit *www.facthound.com*

Type in this code: 9781515766896

 Check out projects, games and lots more at
www.capstonekids.com

INDEX